W9-BSB-862

Let's Explore Japan

by Walt K. Moon

BUMBA BOOKS™

LERNER PUBLICATIONS ◆ MINNEAPOLIS

Note to Educators:

Throughout this book, you'll find critical thinking questions. These can be used to engage young readers in thinking critically about the topic and in using the text and photos to do so.

Lerner Publications Company
A division of Lerner Publishing Group, Inc.
241 First Avenue North
Minneapolis, MN 55401 USA

For reading levels and more information, look up this title at www.lernerbooks.com.

Library of Congress Cataloging-in-Publication Data

Names: Moon, Walt K., author.
Title: Let's explore Japan / by Walt K. Moon.
Description: Minneapolis : Lerner Publications, [2017] | Series: Bumba books™ — Let's explore countries | Includes bibliographical references and index. | Audience: Grades K–3.
Identifiers: LCCN 2016019317 (print) | LCCN 2016019820 (ebook) | ISBN 9781512430080 (lb : alk. paper) | ISBN 9781512430196 (pb : alk. paper) | ISBN 9781512430202 (eb pdf)
Subjects: LCSH: Japan—Juvenile literature.
Classification: LCC DS806 .M617 2016 (print) | LCC DS806 (ebook) | DDC 952—dc23

LC record available at https://lccn.loc.gov/2016019317

Manufactured in the United States of America
1 – VP – 12/31/16

Expand learning beyond the printed book. Download free, complementary educational resources for this book from our website, www.lerneresource.com.

Table of
Contents

A Visit to Japan

Japan is a country in Asia.

The country is made up

of many islands.

Japan has four main islands. Mountains cover the land. Most people live near the sea.

Why do you think most people live near the sea?

Monkeys and foxes live in Japan.

Salmon and tuna swim in its waters.

Japan is known for

cherry trees.

They have pink flowers.

Cherry trees grow all

around the country.

Japan has huge cities.

Tokyo is the biggest.

Thirteen million people

live there.

People from around the world

visit Japan.

They climb mountains.

They shop for electronics in cities.

What else might people buy in cities?

Many Japanese people

eat sushi.

Sushi is made of

rice and fish.

Sushi has vegetables too.

Why do you think Japanese people eat lots of sushi?

Baseball is the biggest

sport in Japan.

People love to watch it.

The top players

are famous.

Japan is a beautiful country.

There are many things to see.

Would you like to visit Japan?

Map of Japan

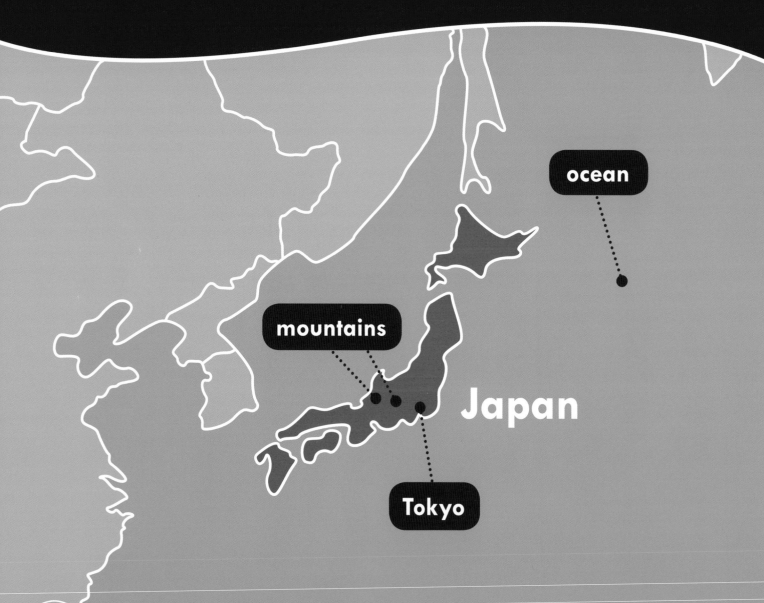

ocean

mountains

Japan

Tokyo

22

Picture Glossary

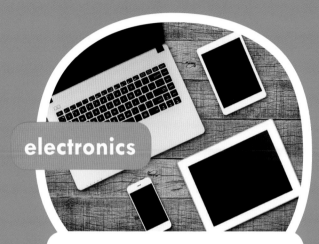

electronics

things that get their power from electricity

islands

pieces of land surrounded by water on all sides

salmon

a fish with pink meat

sushi

a Japanese food made of rice, fish, and vegetables

Index

Read More

Barchers, Suzanne I. *The Tale of the Oki Islands: A Tale from Japan.* South Egremont, MA: Red Chair Press, 2013.

Esbaum, Jill. *Cherry Blossoms Say Spring.* Washington, DC: National Geographic Kids, 2012.

Kuskowski, Alex. *Super Simple Japanese Art: Fun and Easy Art from Around the World.* Minneapolis: Super Sandcastle, 2015.

Photo Credits